Practice Daily Gratitude

Each night write out

3 Things you're thankful for

2 Things you plan to do the next day

1 Thought or action that warmed your heart today

After you've completed your journal, or after writing every 7 days or so , grab a cup of tea or coffee and sit in your favorite spot with a throw blanket and read over all of the things that you have to be thankful for.

In All Things Give Thanks

My Gratitude Journal was created by Arlinda Christine for **LindarInsights LLC** ©2019

My Gratitude Journal

_____
Date

3 Things I'm Grateful For Today

- ♥ _____

- ♥ _____

- ♥ _____

2 Things I Plan To Do Tomorrow

- ♥ _____

- ♥ _____

1 Thing That Warmed My Heart Today

- ♥ _____

_____
Date

3 Things I'm Grateful For Today

- ♥ _____

- ♥ _____

- ♥ _____

2 Things I Plan To Do Tomorrow

- ♥ _____

- ♥ _____

1 Thing That Warmed My Heart Today

- ♥ _____

My Gratitude Journal

3 Things I'm Grateful For Today

- ♥ _____
- ♥ _____
- ♥ _____

2 Things I Plan To Do Tomorrow

- ♥ _____
- ♥ _____

1 Thing That Warmed My Heart Today

- ♥ _____

3 Things I'm Grateful For Today

- ♥ _____
- ♥ _____
- ♥ _____

2 Things I Plan To Do Tomorrow

- ♥ _____
- ♥ _____

1 Thing That Warmed My Heart Today

- ♥ _____

My Gratitude Journal

_____
Date

3 Things I'm Grateful For Today

- ♥ _____
- ♥ _____
- ♥ _____

2 Things I Plan To Do Tomorrow

- ♥ _____
- ♥ _____

1 Thing That Warmed My Heart Today

- ♥ _____

_____
Date

3 Things I'm Grateful For Today

- ♥ _____
- ♥ _____
- ♥ _____

2 Things I Plan To Do Tomorrow

- ♥ _____
- ♥ _____

1 Thing That Warmed My Heart Today

- ♥ _____

My Gratitude Journal

3 Things I'm Grateful For Today

- ♥ _____
- ♥ _____
- ♥ _____

2 Things I Plan To Do Tomorrow

- ♥ _____
- ♥ _____

1 Thing That Warmed My Heart Today

- ♥ _____

Date

3 Things I'm Grateful For Today

- ♥ _____
- ♥ _____
- ♥ _____

2 Things I Plan To Do Tomorrow

- ♥ _____
- ♥ _____

1 Thing That Warmed My Heart Today

- ♥ _____

My Gratitude Journal

_____
Date

3 Things I'm Grateful For Today

- ♥ _____
- ♥ _____
- ♥ _____

2 Things I Plan To Do Tomorrow

- ♥ _____
- ♥ _____

1 Thing That Warmed My Heart Today

- ♥ _____

_____
Date

3 Things I'm Grateful For Today

- ♥ _____
- ♥ _____
- ♥ _____

2 Things I Plan To Do Tomorrow

- ♥ _____
- ♥ _____

1 Thing That Warmed My Heart Today

- ♥ _____

My Gratitude Journal

_____
Date

3 Things I'm Grateful For Today

- ♥ _____
- ♥ _____
- ♥ _____

2 Things I Plan To Do Tomorrow

- ♥ _____
- ♥ _____

1 Thing That Warmed My Heart Today

- ♥ _____

_____
Date

3 Things I'm Grateful For Today

- ♥ _____
- ♥ _____
- ♥ _____

2 Things I Plan To Do Tomorrow

- ♥ _____
- ♥ _____

1 Thing That Warmed My Heart Today

- ♥ _____

My Gratitude Journal

Date _____

3 Things I'm Grateful For Today

- ♥ _____
- ♥ _____
- ♥ _____

2 Things I Plan To Do Tomorrow

- ♥ _____
- ♥ _____

1 Thing That Warmed My Heart Today

- ♥ _____

Date _____

3 Things I'm Grateful For Today

- ♥ _____
- ♥ _____
- ♥ _____

2 Things I Plan To Do Tomorrow

- ♥ _____
- ♥ _____

1 Thing That Warmed My Heart Today

- ♥ _____

My Gratitude Journal

3 Things I'm Grateful For Today

- ♥ _____
- ♥ _____
- ♥ _____

2 Things I Plan To Do Tomorrow

- ♥ _____
- ♥ _____

1 Thing That Warmed My Heart Today

- ♥ _____

_____
Date

3 Things I'm Grateful For Today

- ♥ _____
- ♥ _____
- ♥ _____

2 Things I Plan To Do Tomorrow

- ♥ _____
- ♥ _____

1 Thing That Warmed My Heart Today

- ♥ _____

My Gratitude Journal

_____
Date

3 Things I'm Grateful For Today

- ♥ _____
- ♥ _____
- ♥ _____

2 Things I Plan To Do Tomorrow

- ♥ _____
- ♥ _____

1 Thing That Warmed My Heart Today

- ♥ _____

_____
Date

3 Things I'm Grateful For Today

- ♥ _____
- ♥ _____
- ♥ _____

2 Things I Plan To Do Tomorrow

- ♥ _____
- ♥ _____

1 Thing That Warmed My Heart Today

- ♥ _____

My Gratitude Journal

_____

3 Things I'm Grateful For Today

♥ _____

♥ _____

♥ _____

2 Things I Plan To Do Tomorrow

♥ _____

♥ _____

1 Thing That Warmed My Heart Today

♥ _____

_____
Date

3 Things I'm Grateful For Today

♥ _____

♥ _____

♥ _____

2 Things I Plan To Do Tomorrow

♥ _____

♥ _____

1 Thing That Warmed My Heart Today

♥ _____

My Gratitude Journal

Date _____

3 Things I'm Grateful For Today

- ♥ _____
- ♥ _____
- ♥ _____

2 Things I Plan To Do Tomorrow

- ♥ _____
- ♥ _____

1 Thing That Warmed My Heart Today

- ♥ _____

Date _____

3 Things I'm Grateful For Today

- ♥ _____
- ♥ _____
- ♥ _____

2 Things I Plan To Do Tomorrow

- ♥ _____
- ♥ _____

1 Thing That Warmed My Heart Today

- ♥ _____

My Gratitude Journal

Date

3 Things I'm Grateful For Today

- ♥ _____
- ♥ _____
- ♥ _____

2 Things I Plan To Do Tomorrow

- ♥ _____
- ♥ _____

1 Thing That Warmed My Heart Today

- ♥ _____

_____

Date

3 Things I'm Grateful For Today

- ♥ _____
- ♥ _____
- ♥ _____

2 Things I Plan To Do Tomorrow

- ♥ _____
- ♥ _____

1 Thing That Warmed My Heart Today

- ♥ _____

My Gratitude Journal

_____
Date

3 Things I'm Grateful For Today

♥ _____

♥ _____

♥ _____

2 Things I Plan To Do Tomorrow

♥ _____

♥ _____

1 Thing That Warmed My Heart Today

♥ _____

_____
Date

3 Things I'm Grateful For Today

♥ _____

♥ _____

♥ _____

2 Things I Plan To Do Tomorrow

♥ _____

♥ _____

1 Thing That Warmed My Heart Today

♥ _____

My Gratitude Journal

3 Things I'm Grateful For Today

- ♥ _____
- ♥ _____
- ♥ _____

2 Things I Plan To Do Tomorrow

- ♥ _____
- ♥ _____

1 Thing That Warmed My Heart Today

- ♥ _____

_____
Date

3 Things I'm Grateful For Today

- ♥ _____
- ♥ _____
- ♥ _____

2 Things I Plan To Do Tomorrow

- ♥ _____
- ♥ _____

1 Thing That Warmed My Heart Today

- ♥ _____

My Gratitude Journal

Date

3 Things I'm Grateful For Today

♥ _____

♥ _____

♥ _____

2 Things I Plan To Do Tomorrow

♥ _____

♥ _____

1 Thing That Warmed My Heart Today

♥ _____

Date

3 Things I'm Grateful For Today

♥ _____

♥ _____

♥ _____

2 Things I Plan To Do Tomorrow

♥ _____

♥ _____

1 Thing That Warmed My Heart Today

♥ _____

My Gratitude Journal

_____
Date

3 Things I'm Grateful For Today

- ♥ _____
- ♥ _____
- ♥ _____

2 Things I Plan To Do Tomorrow

- ♥ _____
- ♥ _____

1 Thing That Warmed My Heart Today

- ♥ _____

_____
Date

3 Things I'm Grateful For Today

- ♥ _____
- ♥ _____
- ♥ _____

2 Things I Plan To Do Tomorrow

- ♥ _____
- ♥ _____

1 Thing That Warmed My Heart Today

- ♥ _____

My Gratitude Journal

Date

3 Things I'm Grateful For Today

- ♥ _____
- ♥ _____
- ♥ _____

2 Things I Plan To Do Tomorrow

- ♥ _____
- ♥ _____

1 Thing That Warmed My Heart Today

- ♥ _____

_____
Date

3 Things I'm Grateful For Today

- ♥ _____
- ♥ _____
- ♥ _____

2 Things I Plan To Do Tomorrow

- ♥ _____
- ♥ _____

1 Thing That Warmed My Heart Today

- ♥ _____

My Gratitude Journal

_____
Date

3 Things I'm Grateful For Today

- ♥ _____
- ♥ _____
- ♥ _____

2 Things I Plan To Do Tomorrow

- ♥ _____
- ♥ _____

1 Thing That Warmed My Heart Today

- ♥ _____

_____
Date

3 Things I'm Grateful For Today

- ♥ _____
- ♥ _____
- ♥ _____

2 Things I Plan To Do Tomorrow

- ♥ _____
- ♥ _____

1 Thing That Warmed My Heart Today

- ♥ _____

My Gratitude Journal

3 Things I'm Grateful For Today

- ♥ _____
- ♥ _____
- ♥ _____

2 Things I Plan To Do Tomorrow

- ♥ _____
- ♥ _____

1 Thing That Warmed My Heart Today

- ♥ _____

3 Things I'm Grateful For Today

- ♥ _____
- ♥ _____
- ♥ _____

2 Things I Plan To Do Tomorrow

- ♥ _____
- ♥ _____

1 Thing That Warmed My Heart Today

- ♥ _____

My Gratitude Journal

_____
Date

3 Things I'm Grateful For Today

- ♥ _____
- ♥ _____
- ♥ _____

2 Things I Plan To Do Tomorrow

- ♥ _____
- ♥ _____

1 Thing That Warmed My Heart Today

- ♥ _____

_____
Date

3 Things I'm Grateful For Today

- ♥ _____
- ♥ _____
- ♥ _____

2 Things I Plan To Do Tomorrow

- ♥ _____
- ♥ _____

1 Thing That Warmed My Heart Today

- ♥ _____

My Gratitude Journal

_____
Date

3 Things I'm Grateful For Today

- ♥ _____
- ♥ _____
- ♥ _____

2 Things I Plan To Do Tomorrow

- ♥ _____
- ♥ _____

1 Thing That Warmed My Heart Today

- ♥ _____

_____
Date

3 Things I'm Grateful For Today

- ♥ _____
- ♥ _____
- ♥ _____

2 Things I Plan To Do Tomorrow

- ♥ _____
- ♥ _____

1 Thing That Warmed My Heart Today

- ♥ _____

My Gratitude Journal

_____
Date

3 Things I'm Grateful For Today

- ♥ _____
- ♥ _____
- ♥ _____

2 Things I Plan To Do Tomorrow

- ♥ _____
- ♥ _____

1 Thing That Warmed My Heart Today

- ♥ _____

_____
Date

3 Things I'm Grateful For Today

- ♥ _____
- ♥ _____
- ♥ _____

2 Things I Plan To Do Tomorrow

- ♥ _____
- ♥ _____

1 Thing That Warmed My Heart Today

- ♥ _____

My Gratitude Journal

3 Things I'm Grateful For Today

- ♥ _____
- ♥ _____
- ♥ _____

2 Things I Plan To Do Tomorrow

- ♥ _____
- ♥ _____

1 Thing That Warmed My Heart Today

- ♥ _____

3 Things I'm Grateful For Today

- ♥ _____
- ♥ _____
- ♥ _____

2 Things I Plan To Do Tomorrow

- ♥ _____
- ♥ _____

1 Thing That Warmed My Heart Today

- ♥ _____

My Gratitude Journal

_____
Date

3 Things I'm Grateful For Today

- ♥ _____
- ♥ _____
- ♥ _____

2 Things I Plan To Do Tomorrow

- ♥ _____
- ♥ _____

1 Thing That Warmed My Heart Today

- ♥ _____

_____
Date

3 Things I'm Grateful For Today

- ♥ _____
- ♥ _____
- ♥ _____

2 Things I Plan To Do Tomorrow

- ♥ _____
- ♥ _____

1 Thing That Warmed My Heart Today

- ♥ _____

My Gratitude Journal

_____
Date

3 Things I'm Grateful For Today

- ♥ _____
- ♥ _____
- ♥ _____

2 Things I Plan To Do Tomorrow

- ♥ _____
- ♥ _____

1 Thing That Warmed My Heart Today

- ♥ _____

_____
Date

3 Things I'm Grateful For Today

- ♥ _____
- ♥ _____
- ♥ _____

2 Things I Plan To Do Tomorrow

- ♥ _____
- ♥ _____

1 Thing That Warmed My Heart Today

- ♥ _____

My Gratitude Journal

_____
Date

3 Things I'm Grateful For Today

- ♥ _____
- ♥ _____
- ♥ _____

2 Things I Plan To Do Tomorrow

- ♥ _____
- ♥ _____

1 Thing That Warmed My Heart Today

- ♥ _____

_____
Date

3 Things I'm Grateful For Today

- ♥ _____
- ♥ _____
- ♥ _____

2 Things I Plan To Do Tomorrow

- ♥ _____
- ♥ _____

1 Thing That Warmed My Heart Today

- ♥ _____

My Gratitude Journal

_____
Date

3 Things I'm Grateful For Today

- ♥ _____
- ♥ _____
- ♥ _____

2 Things I Plan To Do Tomorrow

- ♥ _____
- ♥ _____

1 Thing That Warmed My Heart Today

- ♥ _____

_____
Date

3 Things I'm Grateful For Today

- ♥ _____
- ♥ _____
- ♥ _____

2 Things I Plan To Do Tomorrow

- ♥ _____
- ♥ _____

1 Thing That Warmed My Heart Today

- ♥ _____

My Gratitude Journal

_____
Date

3 Things I'm Grateful For Today

- ♥ _____
- ♥ _____
- ♥ _____

2 Things I Plan To Do Tomorrow

- ♥ _____
- ♥ _____

1 Thing That Warmed My Heart Today

- ♥ _____

_____
Date

3 Things I'm Grateful For Today

- ♥ _____
- ♥ _____
- ♥ _____

2 Things I Plan To Do Tomorrow

- ♥ _____
- ♥ _____

1 Thing That Warmed My Heart Today

- ♥ _____

My Gratitude Journal

_____
Date

3 Things I'm Grateful For Today

- ♥ _____
- ♥ _____
- ♥ _____

2 Things I Plan To Do Tomorrow

- ♥ _____
- ♥ _____

1 Thing That Warmed My Heart Today

- ♥ _____

_____
Date

3 Things I'm Grateful For Today

- ♥ _____
- ♥ _____
- ♥ _____

2 Things I Plan To Do Tomorrow

- ♥ _____
- ♥ _____

1 Thing That Warmed My Heart Today

- ♥ _____

My Gratitude Journal

_____
Date

3 Things I'm Grateful For Today

- ♥ _____
- ♥ _____
- ♥ _____

2 Things I Plan To Do Tomorrow

- ♥ _____
- ♥ _____

1 Thing That Warmed My Heart Today

- ♥ _____

_____
Date

3 Things I'm Grateful For Today

- ♥ _____
- ♥ _____
- ♥ _____

2 Things I Plan To Do Tomorrow

- ♥ _____
- ♥ _____

1 Thing That Warmed My Heart Today

- ♥ _____

My Gratitude Journal

_____
Date

3 Things I'm Grateful For Today

- ♥ _____
- ♥ _____
- ♥ _____

2 Things I Plan To Do Tomorrow

- ♥ _____
- ♥ _____

1 Thing That Warmed My Heart Today

- ♥ _____

_____
Date

3 Things I'm Grateful For Today

- ♥ _____
- ♥ _____
- ♥ _____

2 Things I Plan To Do Tomorrow

- ♥ _____
- ♥ _____

1 Thing That Warmed My Heart Today

- ♥ _____

My Gratitude Journal

_____
Date

3 Things I'm Grateful For Today

- ♥ _____
- ♥ _____
- ♥ _____

2 Things I Plan To Do Tomorrow

- ♥ _____
- ♥ _____

1 Thing That Warmed My Heart Today

- ♥ _____

_____
Date

3 Things I'm Grateful For Today

- ♥ _____
- ♥ _____
- ♥ _____

2 Things I Plan To Do Tomorrow

- ♥ _____
- ♥ _____

1 Thing That Warmed My Heart Today

- ♥ _____

My Gratitude Journal

_____
Date

3 Things I'm Grateful For Today

- ♥ _____
- ♥ _____
- ♥ _____

2 Things I Plan To Do Tomorrow

- ♥ _____
- ♥ _____

1 Thing That Warmed My Heart Today

- ♥ _____

_____
Date

3 Things I'm Grateful For Today

- ♥ _____
- ♥ _____
- ♥ _____

2 Things I Plan To Do Tomorrow

- ♥ _____
- ♥ _____

1 Thing That Warmed My Heart Today

- ♥ _____

My Gratitude Journal

_____
Date

3 Things I'm Grateful For Today

- ♥ _____
- ♥ _____
- ♥ _____

2 Things I Plan To Do Tomorrow

- ♥ _____
- ♥ _____

1 Thing That Warmed My Heart Today

- ♥ _____

_____
Date

3 Things I'm Grateful For Today

- ♥ _____
- ♥ _____
- ♥ _____

2 Things I Plan To Do Tomorrow

- ♥ _____
- ♥ _____

1 Thing That Warmed My Heart Today

- ♥ _____

My Gratitude Journal

3 Things I'm Grateful For Today

- ♥ _____
- ♥ _____
- ♥ _____

2 Things I Plan To Do Tomorrow

- ♥ _____
- ♥ _____

1 Thing That Warmed My Heart Today

- ♥ _____

Date

3 Things I'm Grateful For Today

- ♥ _____
- ♥ _____
- ♥ _____

2 Things I Plan To Do Tomorrow

- ♥ _____
- ♥ _____

1 Thing That Warmed My Heart Today

- ♥ _____

My Gratitude Journal

_____
Date

3 Things I'm Grateful For Today

- ♥ _____
- ♥ _____
- ♥ _____

2 Things I Plan To Do Tomorrow

- ♥ _____
- ♥ _____

1 Thing That Warmed My Heart Today

- ♥ _____

_____
Date

3 Things I'm Grateful For Today

- ♥ _____
- ♥ _____
- ♥ _____

2 Things I Plan To Do Tomorrow

- ♥ _____
- ♥ _____

1 Thing That Warmed My Heart Today

- ♥ _____

My Gratitude Journal

_____
Date

3 Things I'm Grateful For Today

- ♥ _____
- ♥ _____
- ♥ _____

2 Things I Plan To Do Tomorrow

- ♥ _____
- ♥ _____

1 Thing That Warmed My Heart Today

- ♥ _____

_____
Date

3 Things I'm Grateful For Today

- ♥ _____
- ♥ _____
- ♥ _____

2 Things I Plan To Do Tomorrow

- ♥ _____
- ♥ _____

1 Thing That Warmed My Heart Today

- ♥ _____

My Gratitude Journal

_____
Date

3 Things I'm Grateful For Today

- ♥ _____

- ♥ _____

- ♥ _____

2 Things I Plan To Do Tomorrow

- ♥ _____

- ♥ _____

1 Thing That Warmed My Heart Today

- ♥ _____

_____
Date

3 Things I'm Grateful For Today

- ♥ _____

- ♥ _____

- ♥ _____

2 Things I Plan To Do Tomorrow

- ♥ _____

- ♥ _____

1 Thing That Warmed My Heart Today

- ♥ _____

My Gratitude Journal

_____
Date

3 Things I'm Grateful For Today

- ♥ _____
- ♥ _____
- ♥ _____

2 Things I Plan To Do Tomorrow

- ♥ _____
- ♥ _____

1 Thing That Warmed My Heart Today

- ♥ _____

_____
Date

3 Things I'm Grateful For Today

- ♥ _____
- ♥ _____
- ♥ _____

2 Things I Plan To Do Tomorrow

- ♥ _____
- ♥ _____

1 Thing That Warmed My Heart Today

- ♥ _____

My Gratitude Journal

_____

Date

3 Things I'm Grateful For Today

- ♥ _____

- ♥ _____

- ♥ _____

2 Things I Plan To Do Tomorrow

- ♥ _____

- ♥ _____

1 Thing That Warmed My Heart Today

- ♥ _____

_____

Date

3 Things I'm Grateful For Today

- ♥ _____

- ♥ _____

- ♥ _____

2 Things I Plan To Do Tomorrow

- ♥ _____

- ♥ _____

1 Thing That Warmed My Heart Today

- ♥ _____

My Gratitude Journal

_____
Date

3 Things I'm Grateful For Today

- ♥ _____
- ♥ _____
- ♥ _____

2 Things I Plan To Do Tomorrow

- ♥ _____
- ♥ _____

1 Thing That Warmed My Heart Today

- ♥ _____

_____
Date

3 Things I'm Grateful For Today

- ♥ _____
- ♥ _____
- ♥ _____

2 Things I Plan To Do Tomorrow

- ♥ _____
- ♥ _____

1 Thing That Warmed My Heart Today

- ♥ _____

My Gratitude Journal

_____
Date

3 Things I'm Grateful For Today

- ♥ _____
- ♥ _____
- ♥ _____

2 Things I Plan To Do Tomorrow

- ♥ _____
- ♥ _____

1 Thing That Warmed My Heart Today

- ♥ _____

_____
Date

3 Things I'm Grateful For Today

- ♥ _____
- ♥ _____
- ♥ _____

2 Things I Plan To Do Tomorrow

- ♥ _____
- ♥ _____

1 Thing That Warmed My Heart Today

- ♥ _____

My Gratitude Journal

3 Things I'm Grateful For Today

- ♥ _____
- ♥ _____
- ♥ _____

2 Things I Plan To Do Tomorrow

- ♥ _____
- ♥ _____

1 Thing That Warmed My Heart Today

- ♥ _____

3 Things I'm Grateful For Today

- ♥ _____
- ♥ _____
- ♥ _____

2 Things I Plan To Do Tomorrow

- ♥ _____
- ♥ _____

1 Thing That Warmed My Heart Today

- ♥ _____

My Gratitude Journal

<u>_____</u>
Date

3 Things I'm Grateful For Today

- ♥ _____
- ♥ _____
- ♥ _____

2 Things I Plan To Do Tomorrow

- ♥ _____
- ♥ _____

1 Thing That Warmed My Heart Today

- ♥ _____

<u>_____</u>
Date

3 Things I'm Grateful For Today

- ♥ _____
- ♥ _____
- ♥ _____

2 Things I Plan To Do Tomorrow

- ♥ _____
- ♥ _____

1 Thing That Warmed My Heart Today

- ♥ _____

My Gratitude Journal

_____
Date

3 Things I'm Grateful For Today

♥ _____

♥ _____

♥ _____

2 Things I Plan To Do Tomorrow

♥ _____

♥ _____

1 Thing That Warmed My Heart Today

♥ _____

_____
Date

3 Things I'm Grateful For Today

♥ _____

♥ _____

♥ _____

2 Things I Plan To Do Tomorrow

♥ _____

♥ _____

1 Thing That Warmed My Heart Today

♥ _____

My Gratitude Journal

_____
Date

3 Things I'm Grateful For Today

- ♥ _____
- ♥ _____
- ♥ _____

2 Things I Plan To Do Tomorrow

- ♥ _____
- ♥ _____

1 Thing That Warmed My Heart Today

- ♥ _____

_____
Date

3 Things I'm Grateful For Today

- ♥ _____
- ♥ _____
- ♥ _____

2 Things I Plan To Do Tomorrow

- ♥ _____
- ♥ _____

1 Thing That Warmed My Heart Today

- ♥ _____

My Gratitude Journal

_____
Date

3 Things I'm Grateful For Today

- ♥ _____
- ♥ _____
- ♥ _____

2 Things I Plan To Do Tomorrow

- ♥ _____
- ♥ _____

1 Thing That Warmed My Heart Today

- ♥ _____

_____
Date

3 Things I'm Grateful For Today

- ♥ _____
- ♥ _____
- ♥ _____

2 Things I Plan To Do Tomorrow

- ♥ _____
- ♥ _____

1 Thing That Warmed My Heart Today

- ♥ _____

My Gratitude Journal

_____
Date

3 Things I'm Grateful For Today

- ♥ _____
- ♥ _____
- ♥ _____

2 Things I Plan To Do Tomorrow

- ♥ _____
- ♥ _____

1 Thing That Warmed My Heart Today

- ♥ _____

_____
Date

3 Things I'm Grateful For Today

- ♥ _____
- ♥ _____
- ♥ _____

2 Things I Plan To Do Tomorrow

- ♥ _____
- ♥ _____

1 Thing That Warmed My Heart Today

- ♥ _____

My Gratitude Journal

_____
Date

3 Things I'm Grateful For Today

- ♥ _____
- ♥ _____
- ♥ _____

2 Things 1 Plan To Do Tomorrow

- ♥ _____
- ♥ _____

1 Thing That Warmed My Heart Today

- ♥ _____

_____
Date

3 Things I'm Grateful For Today

- ♥ _____
- ♥ _____
- ♥ _____

2 Things 1 Plan To Do Tomorrow

- ♥ _____
- ♥ _____

1 Thing That Warmed My Heart Today

- ♥ _____

My Gratitude Journal

_____
Date

3 Things I'm Grateful For Today

- ♥ _____

- ♥ _____

- ♥ _____

2 Things I Plan To Do Tomorrow

- ♥ _____

- ♥ _____

1 Thing That Warmed My Heart Today

- ♥ _____

_____
Date

3 Things I'm Grateful For Today

- ♥ _____

- ♥ _____

- ♥ _____

2 Things I Plan To Do Tomorrow

- ♥ _____

- ♥ _____

1 Thing That Warmed My Heart Today

- ♥ _____

My Gratitude Journal

_____
Date

3 Things I'm Grateful For Today

- ♥ _____
- ♥ _____
- ♥ _____

2 Things I Plan To Do Tomorrow

- ♥ _____
- ♥ _____

1 Thing That Warmed My Heart Today

- ♥ _____

_____
Date

3 Things I'm Grateful For Today

- ♥ _____
- ♥ _____
- ♥ _____

2 Things I Plan To Do Tomorrow

- ♥ _____
- ♥ _____

1 Thing That Warmed My Heart Today

- ♥ _____

My Gratitude Journal

_____
Date

3 Things I'm Grateful For Today

- ♥ _____
- ♥ _____
- ♥ _____

2 Things I Plan To Do Tomorrow

- ♥ _____
- ♥ _____

1 Thing That Warmed My Heart Today

- ♥ _____

_____
Date

3 Things I'm Grateful For Today

- ♥ _____
- ♥ _____
- ♥ _____

2 Things I Plan To Do Tomorrow

- ♥ _____
- ♥ _____

1 Thing That Warmed My Heart Today

- ♥ _____

My Gratitude Journal

_____
Date

3 Things I'm Grateful For Today

- ♥ _____
- ♥ _____
- ♥ _____

2 Things I Plan To Do Tomorrow

- ♥ _____
- ♥ _____

1 Thing That Warmed My Heart Today

- ♥ _____

_____
Date

3 Things I'm Grateful For Today

- ♥ _____
- ♥ _____
- ♥ _____

2 Things I Plan To Do Tomorrow

- ♥ _____
- ♥ _____

1 Thing That Warmed My Heart Today

- ♥ _____

My Gratitude Journal

_____
Date

3 Things I'm Grateful For Today

- ♥ _____

- ♥ _____

- ♥ _____

2 Things I Plan To Do Tomorrow

- ♥ _____

- ♥ _____

1 Thing That Warmed My Heart Today

- ♥ _____

_____
Date

3 Things I'm Grateful For Today

- ♥ _____

- ♥ _____

- ♥ _____

2 Things I Plan To Do Tomorrow

- ♥ _____

- ♥ _____

1 Thing That Warmed My Heart Today

- ♥ _____

My Gratitude Journal

3 Things I'm Grateful For Today

- ♥ _____
- ♥ _____
- ♥ _____

2 Things I Plan To Do Tomorrow

- ♥ _____
- ♥ _____

1 Thing That Warmed My Heart Today

- ♥ _____

3 Things I'm Grateful For Today

- ♥ _____
- ♥ _____
- ♥ _____

2 Things I Plan To Do Tomorrow

- ♥ _____
- ♥ _____

1 Thing That Warmed My Heart Today

- ♥ _____

My Gratitude Journal

_____
Date

3 Things I'm Grateful For Today

- ♥ _____
- ♥ _____
- ♥ _____

2 Things I Plan To Do Tomorrow

- ♥ _____
- ♥ _____

1 Thing That Warmed My Heart Today

- ♥ _____

_____
Date

3 Things I'm Grateful For Today

- ♥ _____
- ♥ _____
- ♥ _____

2 Things I Plan To Do Tomorrow

- ♥ _____
- ♥ _____

1 Thing That Warmed My Heart Today

- ♥ _____

My Gratitude Journal

_____

Date

3 *Things I'm Grateful For Today*

♥ _____

♥ _____

♥ _____

2 *Things I Plan To Do Tomorrow*

♥ _____

♥ _____

1 *Thing That Warmed My Heart Today*

♥ _____

_____

Date

3 *Things I'm Grateful For Today*

♥ _____

♥ _____

♥ _____

2 *Things I Plan To Do Tomorrow*

♥ _____

♥ _____

1 *Thing That Warmed My Heart Today*

♥ _____

My Gratitude Journal

_____
Date

3 Things I'm Grateful For Today

- ♥ _____
- ♥ _____
- ♥ _____

2 Things I Plan To Do Tomorrow

- ♥ _____
- ♥ _____

1 Thing That Warmed My Heart Today

- ♥ _____

_____
Date

3 Things I'm Grateful For Today

- ♥ _____
- ♥ _____
- ♥ _____

2 Things I Plan To Do Tomorrow

- ♥ _____
- ♥ _____

1 Thing That Warmed My Heart Today

- ♥ _____

My Gratitude Journal

_____
Date

3 Things I'm Grateful For Today

- ♥ _____
- ♥ _____
- ♥ _____

2 Things I Plan To Do Tomorrow

- ♥ _____
- ♥ _____

1 Thing That Warmed My Heart Today

- ♥ _____

_____
Date

3 Things I'm Grateful For Today

- ♥ _____
- ♥ _____
- ♥ _____

2 Things I Plan To Do Tomorrow

- ♥ _____
- ♥ _____

1 Thing That Warmed My Heart Today

- ♥ _____

My Gratitude Journal

_____
Date

3 Things I'm Grateful For Today

- ♥ _____
- ♥ _____
- ♥ _____

2 Things I Plan To Do Tomorrow

- ♥ _____
- ♥ _____

1 Thing That Warmed My Heart Today

- ♥ _____

_____
Date

3 Things I'm Grateful For Today

- ♥ _____
- ♥ _____
- ♥ _____

2 Things I Plan To Do Tomorrow

- ♥ _____
- ♥ _____

1 Thing That Warmed My Heart Today

- ♥ _____

My Gratitude Journal

_____

Date

3 Things I'm Grateful For Today

- ♥ _____
- ♥ _____
- ♥ _____

2 Things I Plan To Do Tomorrow

- ♥ _____
- ♥ _____

1 Thing That Warmed My Heart Today

- ♥ _____

_____

Date

3 Things I'm Grateful For Today

- ♥ _____
- ♥ _____
- ♥ _____

2 Things I Plan To Do Tomorrow

- ♥ _____
- ♥ _____

1 Thing That Warmed My Heart Today

- ♥ _____

My Gratitude Journal

_____
Date

3 Things I'm Grateful For Today

- ♥ _____
- ♥ _____
- ♥ _____

2 Things I Plan To Do Tomorrow

- ♥ _____
- ♥ _____

1 Thing That Warmed My Heart Today

- ♥ _____

_____
Date

3 Things I'm Grateful For Today

- ♥ _____
- ♥ _____
- ♥ _____

2 Things I Plan To Do Tomorrow

- ♥ _____
- ♥ _____

1 Thing That Warmed My Heart Today

- ♥ _____

My Gratitude Journal

_____
Date

3 Things I'm Grateful For Today

- ♥ _____

- ♥ _____

- ♥ _____

2 Things I Plan To Do Tomorrow

- ♥ _____

- ♥ _____

1 Thing That Warmed My Heart Today

- ♥ _____

_____
Date

3 Things I'm Grateful For Today

- ♥ _____

- ♥ _____

- ♥ _____

2 Things I Plan To Do Tomorrow

- ♥ _____

- ♥ _____

1 Thing That Warmed My Heart Today

- ♥ _____

My Gratitude Journal

_____
Date

3 Things I'm Grateful For Today

- ♥ _____
- ♥ _____
- ♥ _____

2 Things I Plan To Do Tomorrow

- ♥ _____
- ♥ _____

1 Thing That Warmed My Heart Today

- ♥ _____

_____
Date

3 Things I'm Grateful For Today

- ♥ _____
- ♥ _____
- ♥ _____

2 Things I Plan To Do Tomorrow

- ♥ _____
- ♥ _____

1 Thing That Warmed My Heart Today

- ♥ _____

My Gratitude Journal

_____
Date

3 Things I'm Grateful For Today

- ♥ _____
- ♥ _____
- ♥ _____

2 Things I Plan To Do Tomorrow

- ♥ _____
- ♥ _____

1 Thing That Warmed My Heart Today

- ♥ _____

-
_____
Date

3 Things I'm Grateful For Today

- ♥ _____
- ♥ _____
- ♥ _____

2 Things I Plan To Do Tomorrow

- ♥ _____
- ♥ _____

1 Thing That Warmed My Heart Today

- ♥ _____

My Gratitude Journal

_____
Date

3 Things I'm Grateful For Today

- ♥ _____
- ♥ _____
- ♥ _____

2 Things I Plan To Do Tomorrow

- ♥ _____
- ♥ _____

1 Thing That Warmed My Heart Today

- ♥ _____

_____
Date

3 Things I'm Grateful For Today

- ♥ _____
- ♥ _____
- ♥ _____

2 Things I Plan To Do Tomorrow

- ♥ _____
- ♥ _____

1 Thing That Warmed My Heart Today

- ♥ _____

My Gratitude Journal

Date _____

3 Things I'm Grateful For Today

- ♥ _____
- ♥ _____
- ♥ _____

2 Things I Plan To Do Tomorrow

- ♥ _____
- ♥ _____

1 Thing That Warmed My Heart Today

- ♥ _____

Date _____

3 Things I'm Grateful For Today

- ♥ _____
- ♥ _____
- ♥ _____

2 Things I Plan To Do Tomorrow

- ♥ _____
- ♥ _____

1 Thing That Warmed My Heart Today

- ♥ _____

My Gratitude Journal

_____
Date

3 Things I'm Grateful For Today

- ♥ _____
- ♥ _____
- ♥ _____

2 Things I Plan To Do Tomorrow

- ♥ _____
- ♥ _____

1 Thing That Warmed My Heart Today

- ♥ _____

_____
Date

3 Things I'm Grateful For Today

- ♥ _____
- ♥ _____
- ♥ _____

2 Things I Plan To Do Tomorrow

- ♥ _____
- ♥ _____

1 Thing That Warmed My Heart Today

- ♥ _____

My Gratitude Journal

_____
Date

3 Things I'm Grateful For Today

- ❤ _____
- ❤ _____
- ❤ _____

2 Things I Plan To Do Tomorrow

- ❤ _____
- ❤ _____

1 Thing That Warmed My Heart Today

- ❤ _____

_____
Date

3 Things I'm Grateful For Today

- ❤ _____
- ❤ _____
- ❤ _____

2 Things I Plan To Do Tomorrow

- ❤ _____
- ❤ _____

1 Thing That Warmed My Heart Today

- ❤ _____

My Gratitude Journal

_____
Date

3 Things I'm Grateful For Today

- ♥ _____
- ♥ _____
- ♥ _____

2 Things I Plan To Do Tomorrow

- ♥ _____
- ♥ _____

1 Thing That Warmed My Heart Today

- ♥ _____

_____
Date

3 Things I'm Grateful For Today

- ♥ _____
- ♥ _____
- ♥ _____

2 Things I Plan To Do Tomorrow

- ♥ _____
- ♥ _____

1 Thing That Warmed My Heart Today

- ♥ _____

My Gratitude Journal

_____
Date

3 Things I'm Grateful For Today

- ♥ _____
- ♥ _____
- ♥ _____

2 Things I Plan To Do Tomorrow

- ♥ _____
- ♥ _____

1 Thing That Warmed My Heart Today

- ♥ _____

_____
Date

3 Things I'm Grateful For Today

- ♥ _____
- ♥ _____
- ♥ _____

2 Things I Plan To Do Tomorrow

- ♥ _____
- ♥ _____

1 Thing That Warmed My Heart Today

- ♥ _____

My Gratitude Journal

_____
Date

3 Things I'm Grateful For Today

- ♥ _____
- ♥ _____
- ♥ _____

2 Things I Plan To Do Tomorrow

- ♥ _____
- ♥ _____

1 Thing That Warmed My Heart Today

- ♥ _____

_____
Date

3 Things I'm Grateful For Today

- ♥ _____
- ♥ _____
- ♥ _____

2 Things I Plan To Do Tomorrow

- ♥ _____
- ♥ _____

1 Thing That Warmed My Heart Today

- ♥ _____

My Gratitude Journal

_____
Date

3 Things I'm Grateful For Today

- ♥ _____
- ♥ _____
- ♥ _____

2 Things I Plan To Do Tomorrow

- ♥ _____
- ♥ _____

1 Thing That Warmed My Heart Today

- ♥ _____

_____
Date

3 Things I'm Grateful For Today

- ♥ _____
- ♥ _____
- ♥ _____

2 Things I Plan To Do Tomorrow

- ♥ _____
- ♥ _____

1 Thing That Warmed My Heart Today

- ♥ _____

My Gratitude Journal

_____
Date

3 Things I'm Grateful For Today

- ♥ _____
- ♥ _____
- ♥ _____

2 Things I Plan To Do Tomorrow

- ♥ _____
- ♥ _____

1 Thing That Warmed My Heart Today

- ♥ _____

_____
Date

3 Things I'm Grateful For Today

- ♥ _____
- ♥ _____
- ♥ _____

2 Things I Plan To Do Tomorrow

- ♥ _____
- ♥ _____

1 Thing That Warmed My Heart Today

- ♥ _____

My Gratitude Journal

_____
Date

3 Things I'm Grateful For Today

- ♥ _____
- ♥ _____
- ♥ _____

2 Things I Plan To Do Tomorrow

- ♥ _____
- ♥ _____

1 Thing That Warmed My Heart Today

- ♥ _____

_____
Date

3 Things I'm Grateful For Today

- ♥ _____
- ♥ _____
- ♥ _____

2 Things I Plan To Do Tomorrow

- ♥ _____
- ♥ _____

1 Thing That Warmed My Heart Today

- ♥ _____

My Gratitude Journal

3 Things I'm Grateful For Today

- ♥ _____
- ♥ _____
- ♥ _____

2 Things I Plan To Do Tomorrow

- ♥ _____
- ♥ _____

1 Thing That Warmed My Heart Today

- ♥ _____

Date

3 Things I'm Grateful For Today

- ♥ _____
- ♥ _____
- ♥ _____

2 Things I Plan To Do Tomorrow

- ♥ _____
- ♥ _____

1 Thing That Warmed My Heart Today

- ♥ _____

My Gratitude Journal

_____
Date

3 Things I'm Grateful For Today

- ♥ _____
- ♥ _____
- ♥ _____

2 Things I Plan To Do Tomorrow

- ♥ _____
- ♥ _____

1 Thing That Warmed My Heart Today

- ♥ _____

_____
Date

3 Things I'm Grateful For Today

- ♥ _____
- ♥ _____
- ♥ _____

2 Things I Plan To Do Tomorrow

- ♥ _____
- ♥ _____

1 Thing That Warmed My Heart Today

- ♥ _____

My Gratitude Journal

_____
Date

3 Things I'm Grateful For Today

- ♥ _____
- ♥ _____
- ♥ _____

2 Things I Plan To Do Tomorrow

- ♥ _____
- ♥ _____

1 Thing That Warmed My Heart Today

- ♥ _____

_____
Date

3 Things I'm Grateful For Today

- ♥ _____
- ♥ _____
- ♥ _____

2 Things I Plan To Do Tomorrow

- ♥ _____
- ♥ _____

1 Thing That Warmed My Heart Today

- ♥ _____

My Gratitude Journal

_____
Date

3 Things I'm Grateful For Today

- ♥ _____
- ♥ _____
- ♥ _____

2 Things I Plan To Do Tomorrow

- ♥ _____
- ♥ _____

1 Thing That Warmed My Heart Today

- ♥ _____

_____
Date

3 Things I'm Grateful For Today

- ♥ _____
- ♥ _____
- ♥ _____

2 Things I Plan To Do Tomorrow

- ♥ _____
- ♥ _____

1 Thing That Warmed My Heart Today

- ♥ _____

My Gratitude Journal

_____
Date

3 Things I'm Grateful For Today

- ♥ _____
- ♥ _____
- ♥ _____

2 Things I Plan To Do Tomorrow

- ♥ _____
- ♥ _____

1 Thing That Warmed My Heart Today

- ♥ _____

_____
Date

3 Things I'm Grateful For Today

- ♥ _____
- ♥ _____
- ♥ _____

2 Things I Plan To Do Tomorrow

- ♥ _____
- ♥ _____

1 Thing That Warmed My Heart Today

- ♥ _____

My Gratitude Journal

_____
Date

3 Things I'm Grateful For Today

- ♥ _____
- ♥ _____
- ♥ _____

2 Things I Plan To Do Tomorrow

- ♥ _____
- ♥ _____

1 Thing That Warmed My Heart Today

- ♥ _____

_____
Date

3 Things I'm Grateful For Today

- ♥ _____
- ♥ _____
- ♥ _____

2 Things I Plan To Do Tomorrow

- ♥ _____
- ♥ _____

1 Thing That Warmed My Heart Today

- ♥ _____

My Gratitude Journal

_____
Date

3 Things I'm Grateful For Today

- ♥ _____
- ♥ _____
- ♥ _____

2 Things I Plan To Do Tomorrow

- ♥ _____
- ♥ _____

1 Thing That Warmed My Heart Today

- ♥ _____

_____
Date

3 Things I'm Grateful For Today

- ♥ _____
- ♥ _____
- ♥ _____

2 Things I Plan To Do Tomorrow

- ♥ _____
- ♥ _____

1 Thing That Warmed My Heart Today

- ♥ _____

My Gratitude Journal

_____
Date

3 Things I'm Grateful For Today

- ♥ _____
- ♥ _____
- ♥ _____

2 Things I Plan To Do Tomorrow

- ♥ _____
- ♥ _____

1 Thing That Warmed My Heart Today

- ♥ _____

_____
Date

3 Things I'm Grateful For Today

- ♥ _____
- ♥ _____
- ♥ _____

2 Things I Plan To Do Tomorrow

- ♥ _____
- ♥ _____

1 Thing That Warmed My Heart Today

- ♥ _____

My Gratitude Journal

_____
Date

3 Things I'm Grateful For Today

- ♥ _____
- ♥ _____
- ♥ _____

2 Things I Plan To Do Tomorrow

- ♥ _____
- ♥ _____

1 Thing That Warmed My Heart Today

- ♥ _____

_____
Date

3 Things I'm Grateful For Today

- ♥ _____
- ♥ _____
- ♥ _____

2 Things I Plan To Do Tomorrow

- ♥ _____
- ♥ _____

1 Thing That Warmed My Heart Today

- ♥ _____

My Gratitude Journal

_____
Date

3 Things I'm Grateful For Today

♥ _____

♥ _____

♥ _____

2 Things I Plan To Do Tomorrow

♥ _____

♥ _____

1 Thing That Warmed My Heart Today

♥ _____

_____
Date

3 Things I'm Grateful For Today

♥ _____

♥ _____

♥ _____

2 Things I Plan To Do Tomorrow

♥ _____

♥ _____

1 Thing That Warmed My Heart Today

♥ _____

My Gratitude Journal

_____
Date

3 Things I'm Grateful For Today

- ♥ _____
- ♥ _____
- ♥ _____

2 Things I Plan To Do Tomorrow

- ♥ _____
- ♥ _____

1 Thing That Warmed My Heart Today

- ♥ _____

_____
Date

3 Things I'm Grateful For Today

- ♥ _____
- ♥ _____
- ♥ _____

2 Things I Plan To Do Tomorrow

- ♥ _____
- ♥ _____

1 Thing That Warmed My Heart Today

- ♥ _____

My Gratitude Journal

_____
Date

3 Things I'm Grateful For Today

- ❤ _____
- ❤ _____
- ❤ _____

2 Things I Plan To Do Tomorrow

- ❤ _____
- ❤ _____

1 Thing That Warmed My Heart Today

- ❤ _____

_____
Date

3 Things I'm Grateful For Today

- ❤ _____
- ❤ _____
- ❤ _____

2 Things I Plan To Do Tomorrow

- ❤ _____
- ❤ _____

1 Thing That Warmed My Heart Today

- ❤ _____

My Gratitude Journal

_____
Date

3 Things I'm Grateful For Today

- ♥ _____
- ♥ _____
- ♥ _____

2 Things I Plan To Do Tomorrow

- ♥ _____
- ♥ _____

1 Thing That Warmed My Heart Today

- ♥ _____

_____
Date

3 Things I'm Grateful For Today

- ♥ _____
- ♥ _____
- ♥ _____

2 Things I Plan To Do Tomorrow

- ♥ _____
- ♥ _____

1 Thing That Warmed My Heart Today

- ♥ _____

My Gratitude Journal

Date _____

3 Things I'm Grateful For Today

- ♥ _____
- ♥ _____
- ♥ _____

2 Things I Plan To Do Tomorrow

- ♥ _____
- ♥ _____

1 Thing That Warmed My Heart Today

- ♥ _____

Date _____

3 Things I'm Grateful For Today

- ♥ _____
- ♥ _____
- ♥ _____

2 Things I Plan To Do Tomorrow

- ♥ _____
- ♥ _____

1 Thing That Warmed My Heart Today

- ♥ _____